HEALTH HELPERS

I NEED A DOCTOR

By Rachel Rose

Consultant: Beth Gambro
Reading Specialist, Yorkville, Illinois

BEARPORT
PUBLISHING

Minneapolis, Minnesota

Teaching Tips

Before Reading

- Look at the cover of the book. Discuss the picture and the title.
- Ask readers to brainstorm a list of what they already know about doctors. What can they expect to see in the book?
- Go on a picture walk, looking through the pictures to discuss vocabulary and make predictions about the text.

During Reading

- Read for purpose. Encourage readers to think about the kinds of things that might make us need a doctor.
- Ask readers to look for the details of the book. How can a doctor help?
- If readers encounter an unknown word, ask them to look at the sounds in the word. Then, ask them to look at the rest of the page. Are there any clues to help them understand?

After Reading

- Encourage readers to pick a buddy and reread the book together.
- Ask readers to name two things they might find at a doctor's office. Find the pages that tell about these things.
- Ask readers to write or draw something they learned about doctors as health helpers.

Credits

Cover and title page, © 昊周/Adobe Stock and © luismolinero/Adobe Stock; 3, © luismolinero/Adobe Stock; 5, © Ljupco Smokovski/Adobe Stock, © Khosrork/iStock, and © baona/iStock; 7, © DMP/iStock; 8, © goir/iStock; 9, © RgStudio/iStock; 11, © FatCamera/iStock; 13, © SrdjanPav/iStock; 14, © oceandigital/iStock; 14–15, © YakobchukOlena/iStock; 17, © SDI Productions/iStock and © AaronAmat/iStock; 18–19, © Amorn Suriyan/iStock; 21, © WavebreakMediaMicro/Adobe Stock; 22TL, © Joe_Potato/iStock; 22TR, © stockdevil/iStock; 22MR, © deepblue4you/iStock; © svetikd/iStock; 22BL, © Zerbor/iStock; 22BR, © ktaylorg/iStock; 23TL, © manusapon/Adobe Stock; 23TM, © DeagreeziStock; 23TR, © waxart/Adobe Stock; 23BL, © Kwangmoozaa/iStock; 23BR, © Somsak Thapthimthong/Shutterstock.

See BearportPublishing.com for our statement on Generative AI Usage.

Library of Congress Cataloging-in-Publication Data

Names: Rose, Rachel, 1968- author.
Title: I need a doctor / by Rachel Rose.
Description: Minneapolis, Minnesota : Bearport Publishing Company, [2025] |
 Series: Health helpers | Includes bibliographical references and index.
Identifiers: LCCN 2024021938 (print) | LCCN 2024021939 (ebook) | ISBN
 9798892326339 (library binding) | ISBN 9798892327138 (paperback) | ISBN
 9798892326735 (ebook)
Subjects: LCSH: Physicians--Juvenile literature. | Medical care--Juvenile
 literature.
Classification: LCC R690 .R638 2025 (print) | LCC R690 (ebook) | DDC
 610--dc23/eng/20240701
LC record available at https://lccn.loc.gov/2024021938
LC ebook record available at https://lccn.loc.gov/2024021939

Copyright © 2025 Bearport Publishing Company. All rights reserved. No part of this publication may be reproduced in whole or in part, stored in any retrieval system, or transmitted in any form or by any means, electronic, mechanical, photocopying, recording, or otherwise, without written permission from the publisher.

For more information, write to Bearport Publishing, 5357 Penn Avenue South, Minneapolis, MN 55419.

Contents

A Doctor Helps 4

Doctor Tools............................. 22

Glossary 23

Index 24

Read More 24

Learn More Online....................... 24

About the Author 24

A Doctor Helps

I fell off my bike.

My arm hurts.

Ouch!

Who can help me?

I need a doctor!

A doctor helps people who are hurt or sick.

The doctor's office is busy.

I play with toys as I wait.

Soon, it is my turn.

I sit on a special table.

It can move up and down.

There is a sink by the wall.

I see a first aid kit!

The doctor asks me how I feel.

I tell them my arm hurts.

It is hard to move.

The doctor looks at my arm.

It is **swollen**.

They press on parts of it.

This shows the doctor where my arm hurts the most.

I need an **X-ray**.

Buzz!

This picture shows inside my arm.

I can see my bones!

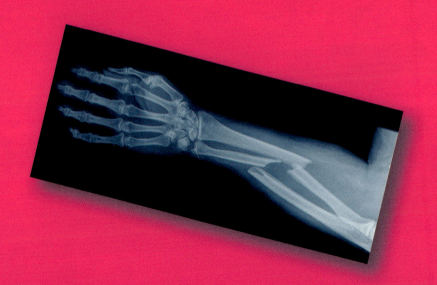

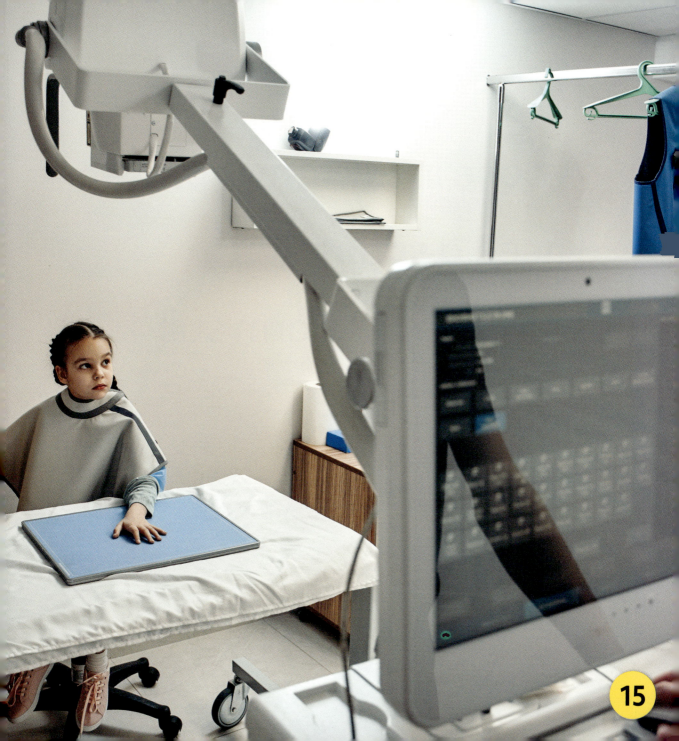

Uh-oh.

A bone in my arm is broken.

I need a **splint**.

It will keep my arm still while it **heals**.

The doctor gives me a splint.

Then, they wrap a **bandage** over it.

This holds the splint in place.

The doctor says I need to be careful.

I cannot ride my bike for a little while.

But I will heal quickly.

Thanks, doctor!

Doctor Tools

A doctor uses many tools.

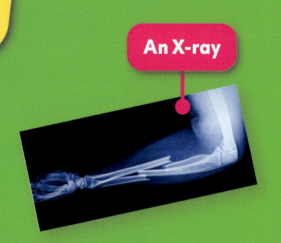
An X-ray

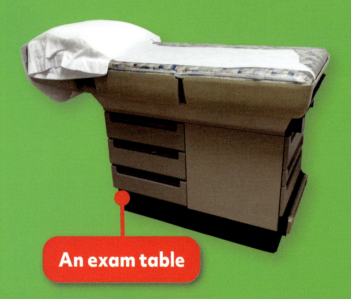
An exam table

A bandage

A first aid kit

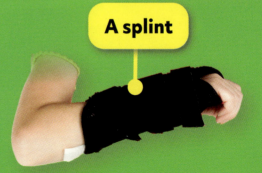
A splint

22

Glossary

bandage a piece of cloth or tape put over a hurt part of the body

heals gets better

splint a cover that helps broken bones mend

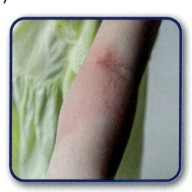

swollen puffy or larger than before

X-ray a picture of the inside of a body

Index

arm 4, 10, 12, 14, 16
bike 4, 20
bones 14, 16
splint 16, 18
table 8
X-ray 14

Read More

Bradley, Doug. *Doctor (I Want to Be a...)*. New York: PowerKids Press, 2023.

Brinker, Spencer. *Doctors (What Makes a Community?)* Minneapolis: Bearport Publishing, 2021.

Learn More Online

1. Go to **FactSurfer.com** or scan the QR code below.
2. Enter "**Need Doctor**" into the search box.
3. Click on the cover of this book to see a list of websites.

About the Author

Rachel Rose goes to the doctor every year for a check-up. This keeps her healthy and happy!